Previous page: The Last Supper *was painted by Leonardo between 1495 and 1497 on the wall of the refectory (dining hall) of the Monastery of Santa Maria delle Grazie in Milan. It was not long after Leonardo had completed the fresco that the colours began to peel off the wall. He had not used the usual fresco technique, but had experimented with a new method, whereby a special varnish is put on the plaster and the colours painted over it. Many attempts have been made to restore the fresco but the greatness of the work, even in its present form, can still be seen.*

Below: Pageants and festivals were part of the life in a Renaissance city. A horse race or Palio like the one below was held in the streets of Florence. This annual celebration was often dangerous. Riders were sometimes thrown and trampled on, and spectators often injured as the horses charged by.

LEONARDO
and His World

Marianne Sachs

Ward Lock Limited · London

Contents

Editorial

Author
Marianne Sachs

Editor
Jane Olliver

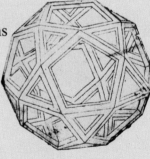

Illustrators
Roger Payne
Roger Phillips

A KINGFISHER BOOK
First published in Great Britain in 1979 by
Ward Lock Limited, 116 Baker Street, London,
W1M 2BB, a Pentos Company.
Designed and produced by Grisewood & Dempsey Limited,
Grosvenor House, 141–143 Drury Lane, London WC2.
© Grisewood & Dempsey Limited 1979

British Library Cataloguing in Publication Data
Sachs, Marianne
    Leonardo and his world. – (Great Masters series)
    1. Leonardo da Vinci – Juvenile literature
    2. Artists – Italy – Biography – Juvenile
    literature.
    I. Title   II. Series
    709'.2'4   ND623.L5
ISBN 0 7063 5868 6
Colour separations by Newsele Litho Limited,
Milan, London.
Printed and bound in Italy by Vallardi Industrie
Grafiche, Milan.

The Renaissance

The Renaissance, a French word meaning *rebirth*, is the name given to the 14th, 15th and 16th centuries. Scholars living during this period of history thought of the Renaissance as a rebirth of learning following the darkness of the Middle Ages. Artists and writers searched for new ways of expressing their new ideas. It was in Italy, with the artist Giotto and the writers Petrarch and Boccaccio, that the Renaissance began. It later spread to the rest of Europe.

Everything that concerned man and his life was of great importance during the Renaissance. This emphasis on the individual formed a philosophy called *humanism* and it was linked to a growing sense of the past. People turned to the ways of life in ancient Greece and Rome as a model. Like the Greeks and Romans they made man the centre of interest.

The Renaissance was a time of new discoveries and inventions in geography, science, astronomy, medicine and printing. It was also a time of great sea voyages of exploration. There were major changes in art which was freed from being merely a craft. Florence, and later Venice and Rome, became important centres. Many great artists emerged, including Michelangelo and Raphael but it is Leonardo da Vinci who stands out. His creative genius not only as a painter, sculptor and architect, but also as a scientist and engineer made him a leading figure of the Renaissance.

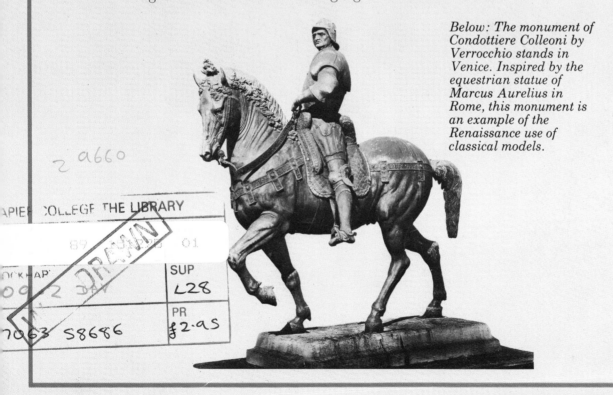

Below: The monument of Condottiere Colleoni by Verrocchio stands in Venice. Inspired by the equestrian statue of Marcus Aurelius in Rome, this monument is an example of the Renaissance use of classical models.

Leonardo's World

In one sense Leonardo's world was an expanding one. It was the age of the great sea explorers and by the 1500s the Americas were discovered, Vasco da Gama had reached India and so opened up the sea route to the valuable trading area of the Indies. But in a more direct sense his world was very enclosed. Travelling was mostly a long, slow business – the limits of speed for the 15th-century man being a horse's pace.

Leonardo's world centred on Florence and Milan. Florence is circled by hills which roll away gently to the south and west. But the traveller journeying north or east would find himself almost at once in the wild rugged mountain country of the Apennines, and the wayfarer would be open to all kinds of hazard. Milan, with its smiling but monotonous approach through the endless Lombard plain must have struck Leonardo as a foreign country. In Renaissance Italy, divided into city-states, a man's city *was* his country. How deeply rooted the feeling must have been in Leonardo's day, for the attitude persists even now. It is remarkable then that Renaissance artists moved with such frequency and apparent ease from one 'country' to another and often over hazardous terrain.

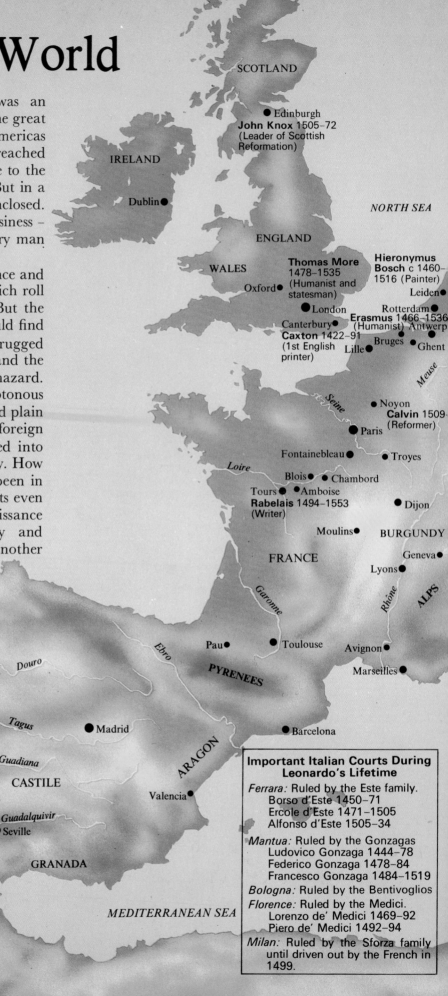

SCOTLAND

Edinburgh
John Knox 1505–72 (Leader of Scottish Reformation)

IRELAND

Dublin

NORTH SEA

ENGLAND

WALES

Oxford

Thomas More 1478–1535 (Humanist and statesman)

London

Canterbury

Caxton 1422–91 (1st English printer)

Hieronymus Bosch c 1460–1516 (Painter)

Leiden

Rotterdam
Erasmus 1466–1536 (Humanist) Antwerp

Bruges
Lille

Ghent

Meuse

Seine

Noyon
Calvin 1509– (Reformer)

Paris

Fontainebleau

Troyes

Loire

Blois

Chambord

Tours

Amboise

Rabelais 1494–1553 (Writer)

Dijon

Moulins

BURGUNDY

FRANCE

Geneva

Lyons

Garonne

Rhône

ALPS

Pau

Toulouse

Avignon

Marseilles

PYRENEES

Douro

PORTUGAL

Tagus

Madrid

Barcelona

Lisbon
Vasco da Gama 1460–1524 (Navigator)
Magellan 1480–1521 (Navigator)
Dias c 1450–1500 (Navigator)

Guadiana

CASTILE

ARAGON

Valencia

Guadalquivir

Seville

GRANADA

MEDITERRANEAN SEA

Ebro

Important Italian Courts During Leonardo's Lifetime

Ferrara: Ruled by the Este family.
Borso d'Este 1450–71
Ercole d'Este 1471–1505
Alfonso d'Este 1505–34

Mantua: Ruled by the Gonzagas
Ludovico Gonzaga 1444–78
Federico Gonzaga 1478–84
Francesco Gonzaga 1484–1519

Bologna: Ruled by the Bentivoglios

Florence: Ruled by the Medici.
Lorenzo de' Medici 1469–92
Piero de' Medici 1492–94

Milan: Ruled by the Sforza family until driven out by the French in 1499.

Stockholm

Lübeck
Hamburg
Bremen
Oder
Vistula
Wittenberg

Danzig
Weser
Thorn
(Torun)
Copernicus 1473–1543
(Astronomer)

Brunswick
Martin Luther 1483–1546
(Reformation leader)

HOLY
Leipzig

Breslau
(Wroclaw)

Frankfurt
Cranach 1472–1553
(Painter)
Prague

POLAND

ROMAN
Nuremberg
Dürer 1471–1528
(Painter)

Augsburg
Holbein, the Elder 1497–1543 (Painter)
Konstanz
Zürich
EMPIRE

Vienna

HUNGARY

Titian 1477–1576
(Painter)
Trento
Brescia
Verona
Venice
G Bellini c 1430–1516
(Painter)
Po
Mantegna 1431–1506 (Painter)
Genoa
Parma
Ferrara
Savonarola 1452–98
(Dominican monk)
Bologna
Danube

ra Angelico 1387–1455
Dominican friar and
ainter)
Pisa
Siena
Florence
Urbino
Raphael 1483–1520
(Painter)
Bramante 1444–1514 (Architect)
Vasari 1511–74
(Art historian
and painter)
Pacioli c 1450–1520
(Franciscan friar
and mathematician)
Rome
Poliziano 1454–94
(Philosopher and
poet)
Naples

FLORENCE
Botticelli 1444–1510
Ghirlandaio 1449–94
(Painters)
Verrocchio 1436–1488
(Painter and sculptor)
Donatello 1386–1466
(Sculptor)
Machiavelli 1469–1527
(Statesman and writer)
Vespucci 1451–1512
(Explorer)
Fra Filippo Lippi
c 1406–69
(Carmelite monk and
painter)
Michelangelo 1475–1564
(Painter, sculptor
and architect)

GENOA
J Cabot 1450–98
(Explorer)
Columbus 1451–1506
(Discoveror of
America)
Alberti 1404–72
(Architect and
painter)
Palermo

MILAN
Po
Pavia
Vicenza
Verona
Mantua
VENICE
Genoa
Parma
Ferrara
Bologna
Pisa
Lucca
Vinci
FLORENCE
Arno
Siena
Arezzo
Urbino
Perugia
Assisi
Tiber
ROME

NAPLES

Palermo

Above: In Leonardo's times Italy was not a unified country as it is today. It consisted of five great city states, Venice, *Milan, Florence, Rome and Naples.*
Below: A map of southern Europe sketched by Leonardo.

Early Years

Below: The village of Vinci where Leonardo was born.

The little village of Vinci lies on the southern slopes of Monte Albano, some 50 kilometres west of Florence. Nestling amongst olive groves and vineyards it has scarcely changed since Leonardo was born there on the 15th of April, 1452.

Leonardo's father, Ser Piero, was a well-known Florentine lawyer. His mother, Catherine, was a poor country girl. She was never married to Ser Piero and so, according to custom, Leonardo was parted from his mother and adopted by his father's family. His childhood was spent in Ser Piero's country estate near Vinci together with his grandparents and his step-mother, Albiera Amadori, the woman Ser Piero had married shortly after Leonardo was born.

Fifteenth-century Florentine society placed great value on education. Leonardo's father ensured that his son learned to read and write and receive a basic knowledge of Latin grammar and mathematics. He learned music too, for we know that he played beautifully on the lute. How early his extraordinary artistic gifts revealed themselves is not certain. But his father took him at the age of 14 to be apprenticed to Andrea Verrocchio, one of the most respected artists in Florence.

Above: Leonardo's earliest known landscape drawing in 1473. It shows the valley of the Arno, possibly near the village of Vinci.

Left: The profile of a warrior in ceremonial armour, about 1480. We see here Leonardo's exquisite draughtsmanship and love of intricate pattern.

10

Below: Several apprentices and assistants were employed by a master artist like Verrocchio. Often the master only did the designs and left the painting to his assistants. Apprentices, the youngest members of the workshop, would be put to such tasks as the grinding of pigments. The sculpture we see is Verrocchio's Boy with Dolphin, about 1475.

Above: The Annunciation, in the Uffizi in Florence, was painted by Leonardo while he was working in Verrocchio's shop in about 1472. The annunciating angel is modelled in Leonardo's new technique of chiaroscuro (light and shade). By this means the artist emphasized the mass and surface of the form rather than its outlines.

Right: A detail from Verrocchio's Baptism of Christ, painted in about 1472, shows a kneeling angel in profile. The angel was painted by Leonardo while he was working in Verrocchio's workshop. The art historian Vasari wrote that Verrocchio was so stunned by his pupil's success that he never wanted to paint again.

Fifteenth-Century Florence

The 15th century opened on a desperate note for the Florentines. In 1402 they prepared themselves to be wiped out by the invading forces of the Milanese lords, the Visconti, sweeping down from the north. But the Milanese leader, Giangaleazzo, suddenly died and Florence was reprieved. Fiercely proud of its Republican status, this narrow escape reinforced Florence's strong spirit of freedom and determination to keep invaders from the door. The Florentine economy was built on banking and trade. It was in the city's interest to keep internal peace and stability. This sentiment is reflected in a letter from a merchant Datini, dated 1404, while Florence was still suffering the effects of her recent upheavals. Datini writes 'God grant us peace soon, so that merchandize can again come and go as it should; it seems a thousand years [that we have been at war]'.

The great commissions of sculpture that characterize Florentine art in the first part of the 15th century are an expression of pride in the Republican state. But they also show the growing humanist influence in Florence with its emphasis on the importance of man. However, when Cosimo de' Medici acquired so much financial power within the Signoria or city council, in the 1430s, the fervent Republicanism of the early years slowly began to dwindle. By the time Lorenzo emerged as the head of state in 1469, Florentine humanists like the poets Poliziano and Pico della Mirandola had lost this sense of public-spiritedness.

Above: Masaccio's supreme draughtsmanship and classical style are shown in his Tribute Money, *about 1426–27. The painting is part of a fresco cycle showing the life of St Peter.*

Below: A view of 15th-century Florence looking north across the Arno river to the Fiesole hills. On the left, the huge cathedral with Brunelleschi's dome and Giotto's bell-tower dwarfs the surrounding houses. On the right is the Palazzo Vecchio, seat of the Republican government. The famous bridge, the Ponte Vecchio, crosses the Arno in the foreground.

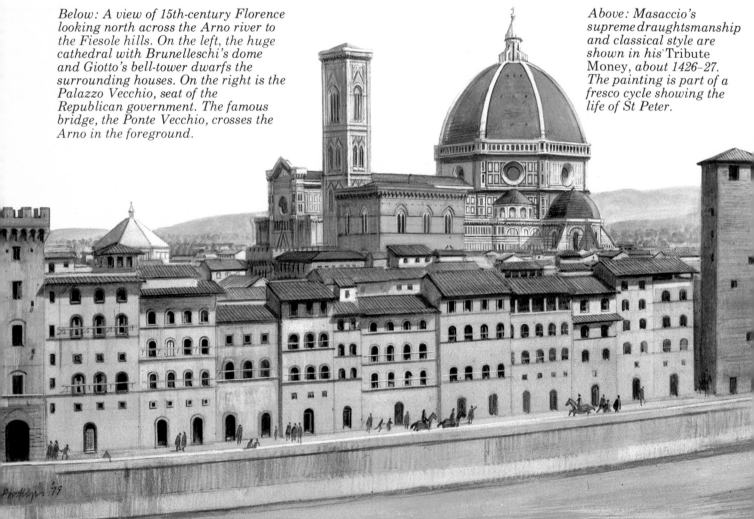

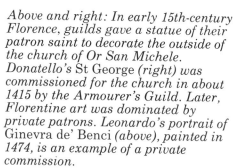

Above and right: In early 15th-century Florence, guilds gave a statue of their patron saint to decorate the outside of the church of Or San Michele. Donatello's St George (right) was commissioned for the church in about 1415 by the Armourer's Guild. Later, Florentine art was dominated by private patrons. Leonardo's portrait of Ginevra de' Benci (above), painted in 1474, is an example of a private commission.

The Renaissance Man

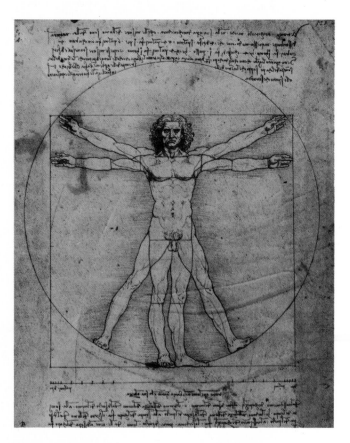

Vitruvian man (see left) reflects the spirit in which the Renaissance individual experienced himself. Leonardo's drawing is taken from the architectural treatise by the Roman Vitruvius. This book enabled Renaissance artists to study the system of perfect proportions on which classical architectural practice is based. For the 15th- and 16th-century Florentines, man was spiritually, intellectually and physically at the centre of his Earth. He was no longer at the mercy of natural forces but looking for ways to control them. In his quest for greater understanding and knowledge he strove towards every aspect of life. By the end of the 15th century it was not uncommon to find men, like Fracastoro, trained in medicine, but equally at home with Ciceronian Latin or current architectural theory. Leonbattista Alberti and Leonardo are two other outstanding examples of this universality. Women, too, played an important role and there is no better example of the intelligent and cultured Renaissance woman than Isabella d'Este, daughter of Ercole d'Este and his wife Leonora of Aragon. Isabella was a brilliant writer and a great patron of the arts.

Above: Leonardo's drawing of the proportions of the human figure is based on the classical writings of Vitruvius. It demonstrates the perfection of man's proportions which can be inscribed in a circle or a square. It is the most famous of Leonardo's measurement drawings.

Above, from left to right: Ludovico Sforza, Duke of Milan and patron of Leonardo; Lorenzo de' Medici (the Magnificent). Florentine statesman; Michelangelo, sculptor and painter; and Machiavelli, writer and statesman.

Left: This fresco by Domenico Ghirlandaio shows Honorius III bestowing the Franciscan Order on St Francis. The figures in the foreground are Lorenzo de' Medici and members of the Medici family.

Above left: The detail of the Three Graces from Botticelli's Primavera *(Spring) reflects the influence of Classical images on Renaissance art. It was painted in about 1477.*

Left: The magnificent dome of St Peter's Basilica was designed by Michelangelo.

Above: Raphael's Belle Jardinière, *dated 1507, is one of a series of Madonna pictures which Raphael painted in Florence.*

Below: Secular or non-religious paintings were increasingly in demand in the Renaissance. Paolo Uccello's hunting scene was painted some time after 1460 to decorate a marriage chest.

Above: The cartoon of the Adoration of the Magi *was painted for the monks at San Donato at Scopeto. It was left unfinished when Leonardo went to Milan in 1482. The underpainting in neutral colours of greys, browns, blacks and whites shows clearly Leonardo's method of chiaroscuro modelling.*

Below: Leonardo's drawing of a polyhedron for Fra Luca Pacioli's book On Divine Proportion.

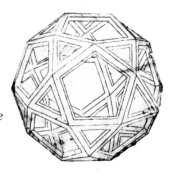

Left: This lined, perspective drawing is a detail of Leonardo's study for the Adoration of the Magi.

The Milanese Court

The style of the Milanese court which Leonardo entered in 1482 was extravagant and pleasure-seeking. Unlike Florence, which had always prided itself on its Republican spirit, Milan was a city run by warrior tyrants.

Leonardo's patron, Ludovico Sforza, was cast in the same tough and wily mould as his forebears. His father, Francesco, had become the ruler of Milan by marrying the daughter of one of the previous Milanese lords. It was mainly through Francesco that Milan achieved military power and financial prosperity to rival any of the Italian city-states. The splendour of Ludovico's court showed the wealth and importance that the Sforza family had achieved for Milan.

Much of Leonardo's time at the Milanese court was occupied in designing war machinery. But his engineering skills were also put to more homely uses, such as designs for the installation of central heating. Leonardo considered his work as an engineer to be far more important than his work as an artist. Apart from the great fresco of the *Last Supper* (see end pages) only a few of Leonardo's great paintings emerged during the eighteen years spent in Milan.

Above: Lady with an Ermine, *Leonardo's portrait of Cecilia Gallerani, Ludovico Sforza's mistress, was painted about 1483.*
Below: Court musicians and acrobats provided entertainment in the Sforza court in Milan.

Master Artist in Florence

When Leonardo returned to Florence for six years in 1500, after the fall of Ludovico Sforza, his reputation as a painter was at its height. He was nearly 50 years old, and many changes had occurred during the two decades of his absence. A new generation of artists had grown up. Michelangelo Buonarroti, now 25, came home to Florence in 1501, fresh from his success as a sculptor in Rome. Leonardo and Michelangelo, two artistic giants, found themselves together for the first time in their native city. Their rivalry is legendary. Shortly before Michelangelo's return, Leonardo had made a cartoon, that is, a highly finished drawing, of the *Virgin and Child with St Anne.* He put it on display in the Church of Santissima Annunziata and the 16th-century historian Vasari tells us that 'Leonardo's masterpiece astonished the entire population'. Not long after this, between 1503 and 1506, he painted his famous portrait of the *Mona Lisa.*

Michelangelo soon had his chance to place his own genius beside that of the older master where all could see it. In 1503 Leonardo was commissioned by the new Republican government to decorate one wall of the council chamber in the Palazzo della Signoria. The fresco was to commemorate the famous Florentine victory of 1441 over the Milanese, the Battle of Anghiari. Michelangelo was asked the next year to paint the wall opposite. His theme was the Battle of Cascina. But both compositions were doomed to be left unfinished. Leonardo's new method of applying oils to plaster failed and Michelangelo's work was interrupted by a summons from Pope Julius II to go to Rome. This theme of frustrated endings was to haunt both artists throughout their lives.

Left: Leonardo's study of a man shouting for the Battle of Anghiari *fresco.*

Far left: Leonardo's oil painting of the Virgin and Child with St Anne, *a later version of the cartoon displayed in Florence.*

Right: Leonardo's famous portrait of the Mona Lisa.

Below: A copy of Leonardo's cartoon of the Battle of Anghiari.

The Vision of a Genius

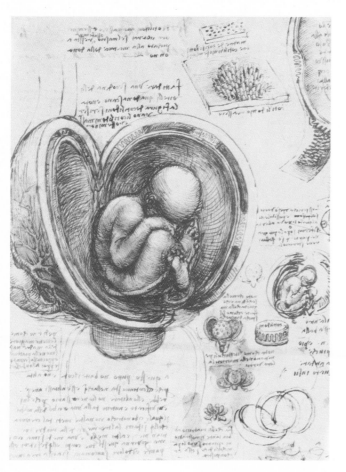

Leonardo's genius lies in a rare combination of powers. There were many Renaissance artists who could turn with ease from painting a Madonna picture to designing an equestrian monument. But who could turn from the study of the flight of birds and then apply himself to the problem of diverting the course of a river? Who could draw the most acutely observed series of caricatures and then paint the most beautiful Madonna? If the range of Leonardo's interests is staggering, so also is the range of his expression. We have only to look at the *Last Supper* to see this – how a quiet figure is placed beside a highly agitated one to the great enhancement of each. This love of contrast is reflected in several sheets of drawings where an old or ugly face appears beside a young or beautiful one. Leonardo's drawing and painting also show the intensity of his feeling for organic life and the superhuman quality of his eye. His sight was so swift that he could see aspects of objects which only the camera is normally able to capture.

During the first part of his life Leonardo's scientific activities served his artistic imagination. After the *Battle of Anghiari* fresco his scientific interests came first and his draughtsmanship became simply a tool in these studies.

Above: Leonardo's drawing of an embryo in the womb was done between about 1510–1512. His studies in anatomy show a detailed knowledge of the human body, acquired by dissecting corpses.

Right: Study of an old face reflects Leonardo's interest in grotesque and fantastic forms.

Far right: Animals and plants interested Leonardo as much as the human body. This drawing shows his study of violas, about 1487.

Right: Sketch of a prancing horse, about 1511.

Far right: Study of a cat. Leonardo drew sketches of many other animals, including dogs, lions, crabs, oxen and eagles.

Right: The Madonna of the Rocks. *There are two versions of this picture. The first, shown here, was painted between 1483 and 1485. Charles d'Amboise took it back to France for the king, and it now hangs in the Louvre, Paris. The later version done to replace it is in the National Gallery, London. The Louvre painting is very much in the style of Leonardo's earliest Florentine period with its soft and glowing colours. The fantastic rock formations in the background are typical of Leonardo's landscapes with his love of vertical forms.*

Below: Architecture was of great interest to Leonardo. The sketch shows a design for a double staircase, drawn between 1487–1490.

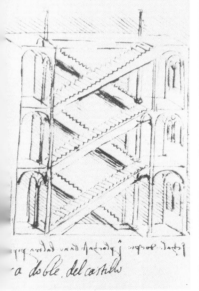

21

Leonardo the Inventor

In a letter to Ludovico Sforza in 1481 Leonardo boasted that he could construct all sorts of war weapons. Amongst other things he said that he could 'demolish fortresses built on rocks' and could make 'a kind of bombard which hurls showers of small stones and the smoke of which strikes terror into the enemy'. Of all his military engineering designs the drawing of cannon balls exploding in mid-flight (see right) fits most closely to this description.

We should not be surprised to find so much of Leonardo's time taken up with designing war machinery, for during the 15th and 16th centuries war was considered an art. The designing of weapons required a high degree of draughtsmanship. Many of Leonardo's drawings of weapons were done in the first five years at the Sforza court in Milan. But weapons were not the only brilliant inventions to come from Leonardo. His interests in the principles of hydraulics and pulley systems occupied him throughout his life. He had detailed plans for making canals with locks for transporting goods and for irrigation. Aerodynamics was another source for his inventive imagination. His extraordinarily accurate studies of the flight of birds led him to devise various flying machines. He also invented cutting machines, soldering tools, treadle-operated lathes and mechanical saws. But it is difficult to tell how functional his more ambitious and grandiose schemes really were. Possibly some, like his drawings for a crossbow, were too advanced for the techniques of that time. Others, like his designs for halberds, seem to have had a more ornamental than practical purpose.

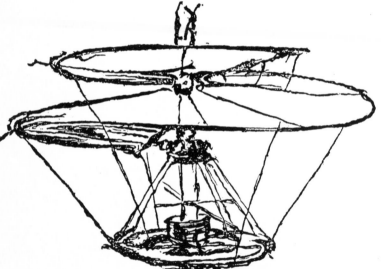

Far left: A design for a flying machine. Leonardo's studies for flying machines came from his great desire to imitate bird flight.

Left: Leonardo's drawing of a parachute.

Below: Leonardo's design for a canal dredger. He made plans for canal systems with locks for transport and irrigation.

Below: Leonardo's inventive genius stretched to designs for walking on water by means of floats attached to the feet.

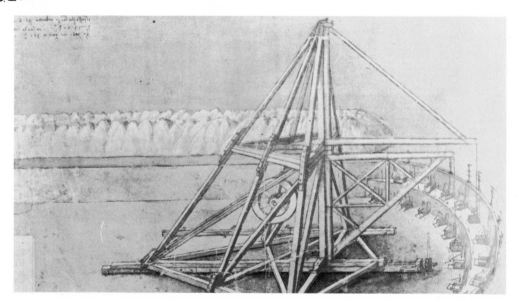

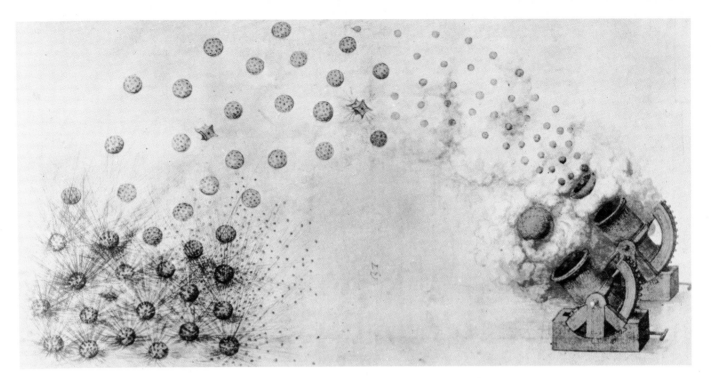

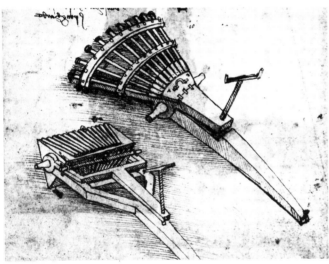

Above: An example of
Leonardo's military
expertise can be seen in
this design for explosive
mortar bombs.

Below left: A drawing for
a large crossbow on a
carriage with inclined
wheels.

Left: Leonardo's designs
for multi-barrelled guns.

Below: Using his
knowledge of pulleys,
Leonardo invented a
device for pushing down
scaling ladders during a
siege.

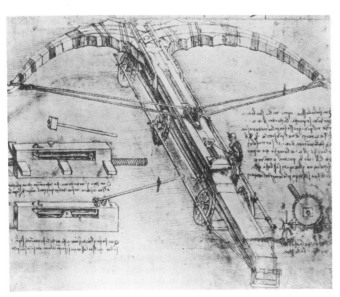

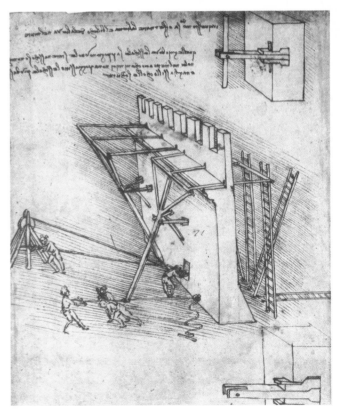

23

The Last Years

L eonardo's elusive personality became even more obvious during old age. He left Milan for Rome in 1513 and was given rooms by Giuliano de' Medici, the Pope's brother, in the Belvedere Palace of the Vatican.

Few details of his life here survive. The blurred picture which emerges shows us only a venerable old man who remained aloof from the exciting, but formidable, artistic world around him. Most of his time seemed to be spent devising all sorts of geometric and optical puzzles, or experimenting with new kinds of varnish and oils for painting. Several drawings of awe-inspiring events can be dated to the period of this Roman sojourn. They reveal Leonardo's obsessive fascination with the devastating power of nature. He envisaged a series of destructive events such as a mountain falling on a town and the rage of a deluge at its height.

Though the great papal commissions completed by Michelangelo and Raphael had little effect on the older master, Leonardo's mere presence in Rome made an impact on the younger generation.

Soon after Giuliano de' Medici died in 1516, Leonardo was invited to the court of the new French king, Francis I. Again Leonardo produced virtually nothing. The French monarch seems to have valued him most for his companionship and brilliant conversation. And so Leonardo passed the last three years of life in the refined and quiet atmosphere of a court far from his native land. He died on the 2nd of May, 1519 at the little castle of Cloux, near Amboise, a gift he had received from the king on his arrival in France.

Above: The little castle of Cloux near Amboise in France where Leonardo spent his final years. He died there on 2nd May 1519. Today the house has been restored to almost the state in which it was when Leonardo lived there.

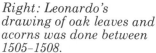

Right: Leonardo's drawing of oak leaves and acorns was done between 1505–1508.

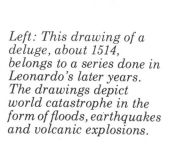

Left: This drawing of a deluge, about 1514, belongs to a series done in Leonardo's later years. The drawings depict world catastrophe in the form of floods, earthquakes and volcanic explosions.

Left: St John the Baptist, *from Leonardo's late period, is his most dramatic expression of chiaroscuro.*

Below: Leonardo's self-portrait. This red chalk drawing, about 1512, is the only known authentic likeness of the artist.

Time Chart

Year	Leonardo's Life	Other Events
1452	Birth of Leonardo da Vinci.	Birth of Savonarola.
1453		Constantinople falls to the Turks; Hundred Years' War ends between France and England.
1454		Printing with movable type is perfected in Germany by Johannes Gutenberg.
1458		Pius II (Aeneas Sylvius Piccolomini) becomes Pope.
1461		Edward IV becomes King of England; Louis XI becomes King of France.
1464		Paul II (Pietro Barbo) becomes Pope.
1466	Probable date of apprenticeship with Andrea del Verrocchio in Florence.	Birth of Erasmus; Death of Donatello.
1469		Birth of Machiavelli; Marriage between Ferdinand of Aragon and Isabella of Castile creates the new national state of Spain; Lorenzo de' Medici comes to power in Florence; Death of Fra Filippo Lippi.
1471		Sixtus IV (Francesco della Rovere) becomes Pope; Birth of Albrecht Dürer.
1472	Joins the Florentine Guild of Artists; Continues to work in Verrocchio's shop; Paints the angel on the left in Verrocchio's *Baptism of Christ*; Probable date of his painting of the *Annunciation*.	
1473	Draws the landscape sketch of the Arno valley.	Birth of Nicolaus Copernicus; Building of the Sistine Chapel begun by Giovanni de Dolci; Sandro Botticelli employed by the Medici.
1474	Portrait of *Ginevra de' Benci*, possibly in celebration of her marriage in January.	William Caxton prints the first book in English.
1475		Birth of Michelangelo Buonarotti; Vatican Library open to the public; Oil technique of painting introduced to Venice, probably by Antonella da Messina.
1476	Leonardo is thought to have left Verrocchio with whom he has lived until that date.	
1478	He begins painting the *Benois Madonna* and a series of drawings of *Madonna with a Cat*. He receives an important independent commission, the altarpiece in the Chapel of St Bernard in the Signoria (city council) in Florence, but never painted it; Earliest drawings of war machinery.	Birth of Thomas More; Pazzi Conspiracy against the Medici fails.
1480	Paints the *Madonna Litta* and probable date of the sketch of a warrior in ceremonial armour.	Birth of Ferdinand Magellan.
1481	Commissioned to do the *Adoration of the Magi* from the monks of San Donato at Scopeta; He writes a letter of self-recommendation to Ludovico Sforza.	Botticelli, Perugino and Ghirlandaio called to Rome to paint the Sistine Chapel frescoes.
1482	Leonardo leaves Florence for Milan; From about this date he keeps notebooks.	Sistine Chapel frescoes completed.
1483	Contracted by the Confraternity of the Immaculate Conception to paint the *Madonna of the Rocks*; Probable date of portrait of Cecilia Gallerani (*Lady with an Ermine*); Begins studies for the Sforza equestrian monument.	Birth of Martin Luther and Raphael; Death of Edward IV of England and Louis XI of France; Charles VIII becomes King of France; Introduction of oils to Florence with the arrival of Hugo van der Goes' *Portinari* altarpiece.
1484		Death of Pope Sixtus IV; Innocent VIII becomes Pope.
1485	Probable date of *Portrait of a Musician*.	Henry VII becomes King of England.
1488	Study for Sforza monument; Model for central lantern of Duomo in Milan; Drawings of churches and artificial flight.	Bartholomew Dias rounds the Cape of Good Hope; Death of Verrocchio.
1489	Earliest sheet of anatomical drawings of skulls, dated by Leonardo as 5th April of that year.	Savonarola becomes Prior of San Marco, Florence.
1492		Christopher Columbus discovers America; Death of Pope Innocent VIII and Lorenzo de' Medici; Alexander VI (Roderigo Borgia) becomes Pope; Piero de' Medici comes to power in Florence.

Year	Leonardo's Life	Other Events
1493	Model horse for the Sforza monument exhibited on the occasion of Bianco Maria Sforza's marriage to the Emperor Maximilian.	Maximilian I becomes Holy Roman Emperor.
1494	Leonardo teaches himself Latin.	Birth of Rabelais; Charles VIII of France invades Italy; Fall of the Medici in Florence, Savonarola comes to power; Michelangelo in Venice and Bologna.
1495	Probable date of the contract for the *Last Supper*.	Naples falls to Charles VIII.
1496	The mathematician Luca Pacioli arrives in Milan.	French are ousted from Naples by Spanish troops; Michelangelo goes to Rome; Plague breaks out in Florence.
1497	The *Last Supper* finished; Works with Pacioli on his book *On Divine Proportions*; Between 1497 and 1499 Leonardo probably drew the cartoon of the *Virgin and Child with St Anne*, known as the Burlington House Cartoon.	John and Sebastian Cabot reach the east coast of North America; Savonarola excommunicated.
1498	Leonardo is given property by Ludovico Sforza outside Porta Vercellina, Milan.	Death of Charles VIII; Louis XII becomes King of France; Savonarola burned at the stake; Vasco da Gama discovers the sea route to the Indies.
1499	The French enter Milan and Leonardo leaves for Mantua where he draws Isabella d'Estes' portrait. He goes to Venice in March of that year.	Louis XII invades Italy and conquers Milan; Amerigo Vespucci leaves Spain on voyage of discovery to South America.
1500	Leonardo returns to Florence in April.	The French take Milan for a second time and capture Ludovico Sforza at Novara; Vasco da Gama returns home.
1501	Exhibits a cartoon of the *Virgin and Child with St Anne* in the Church of the Santissima Annunziata.	Michelangelo returns to Florence and works on *David*.
1502	Leonardo is employed by Cesare Borgia.	War breaks out between France and Spain.
1503	Leonardo is commissioned to do the fresco of the *Battle of Anghiari*; Sometime between 1503 and 1506 he paints the *Mona Lisa*.	Death of Pope Alexander VI, his son Cesare Borgia loses political power; Julius II (Giuliano della Rovere) becomes Pope, after 26-day reign of Pius III (Piccolomini).
1506	He takes leave of the Signoria for short stay in Milan.	Death of Andrea Mantegna and Columbus; Donato Bramante draws design for St Peter's; Julius II conquers Bologna.
1507	Returns to Florence briefly in the autumn on his father's death; On his return to Milan his chief patron becomes Charles d'Amboise.	Martin Luther ordained.
1508	Makes some architectural drawings and the studies of the corrosion of buildings; A series of notes on botany, geology, atmosphere and landscape probably dates from this period.	Michelangelo starts ceiling of Sistine Chapel; Raphael goes to Rome; League of Cambrai with the Pope and allies against Venice.
1510	Probable date of the painting of *Virgin and Child with St Anne* (Louvre version).	Death of Botticelli; Luther in Rome; Erasmus in Cambridge.
1511	Charles d'Amboise dies and is succeeded by Gaston de Foix and Gian Giacomo Trivulzio; Draws masquerade costumes and the *Embryo in the Womb*.	Pope Julius II forms Holy League with Venice, England and Aragon to drive the French out of Italy; Birth of Giorgio Vasari.
1512	Probable date of Leonardo's self-portrait.	French defeat the Spanish and papal forces at Ravenna; Medici power is restored in Florence; Michelangelo finishes work on Sistine Chapel.
1513	Leonardo leaves Milan for Rome together with his assistants; His patron is Giuliano de' Medici, brother of Pope Leo X.	Death of Pope Julius II; Giovanni de' Medici, son of Lorenzo de' Medici becomes Pope Leo X; Machiavelli begins the *Prince*.
1514	Leonardo makes a brief visit to Parma. Probable date of the series of deluge drawings.	Death of Bramante; Raphael put in charge of antiquities in Rome.
1515	Probable date of *St John the Baptist*.	Francis I becomes King of France and invades Italy.
1516	He leaves Italy for France on the death of Giuliano de' Medici and is given the gift of the Castle at Cloux, Amboise.	Michelangelo returns to Florence to work for the Medici; Death of Giovanni Bellini and Hieronymus Bosch; Thomas More's *Utopia* published.
1517	Leonardo receives a visit from the Cardinal of Aragon to whom he shows his last works.	The Reformation begins with Luther nailing his 95 Theses to the church door at Wittenberg.
1519	Leonardo dies at Cloux on May 2nd.	Mannerist style of painting emerges in Italy; Magellan begins voyage around the world.

Leonardo's Greatest Works

Paintings: The *Adoration of the Magi* Oil on panel, 258 × 243 cm, Uffizi Gallery, Florence (c 1481).

The *Madonna of the Rocks* Oil on panel transferred to canvas, 190 × 120 cm, Louvre, Paris (1483).

The *Madonna of the Rocks* Oil on panel, 189 × 120 cm, National Gallery, London (c 1506).

Last Supper Fresco, 910 × 420 cm, Santa Maria delle Grazie, Milan (c 1495–97).

Virgin and Child with St Anne Oil on panel, 170 × 129 cm, Louvre, Paris (c 1510).

St John the Baptist Oil on panel, 69 × 57 cm, Louvre, Paris (c 1515).

Portrait of the *Mona Lisa* Oil on panel, 77 × 53 cm, Louvre, Paris (c 1503–1506).

Annunciation Oil on panel, 217 × 98 cm, Uffizi Gallery, Florence (c 1472).

Lady with an Ermine Oil on panel, 55 × 40 cm, Museum Czartoryski, Cracow (1483).

Portrait of *Ginevra de' Benci* Oil on panel, 42 × 37 cm, National Gallery, Washington (1474).

Drawings: Cartoon of the *Virgin and Child with St Anne and the Infant St John the Baptist* Black chalk, 139 × 100 cm, Burlington House, London (c 1497).

Arno Landscape Pen and ink, 28 × 19 cm, Uffizi, Florence (1473).

Profile of a *Warrior* Silverpoint, 28 × 20 cm, British Museum, London (c 1480).

Studies for the *Battle of Anghiari* Pen and ink, Museum of Fine Arts, Budapest (c 1503).

Embryo in the Womb Pen and ink, 47 × 33 cm, Royal Collection, Windsor Castle (1511).

Grotesque heads Pen and ink, Royal Collection, Windsor Castle.

Studies of *Horses for St George and the Dragon* Pen and ink, Royal Collection, Windsor Castle.

Study for the *Madonna Litta* Silverpoint, 18 × 17 cm, Louvre, Paris (1480).

Deluge drawings Chalk with ink, Royal Collection, Windsor Castle (1514–16).

Self-portrait Red chalk, 33 × 21 cm, Biblioteca Reale, Turin (c 1512).

Studies of *Leda and Swan* Pen and ink over black chalk, Royal Collection, Windsor Castle (c 1504).

Glossary

Anatomy The science of the structure of the body.

Cartoon A highly finished preliminary drawing or sketch for copying later as a painting or a *fresco*.

Chiaroscuro Contrasts of light and shade in a picture.

Classical art A style of art, derived from ancient Greece and ancient Rome, governed by rules based on reason, order and balance. Classical artists tended to use geometric forms.

Condottiere The leader of a mercenary group of soldiers in Italy.

Equestrian statue A monument of a horse and rider, particularly popular during the 15th and 16th centuries.

Fresco A wall painting made by applying paints to freshly laid plaster. The true fresco is *al fresco* (applying colour to wet plaster), but many wall paintings are made by putting colour on a dry surface, called *al secco*. This method was less skilful and less enduring than *al fresco*.

Guild A union of craftsmen which kept standards of work high and looked after the interests of its members.

Humanism A movement which emphasizes the importance of man, his interests and his place in the world. Humanism, with its roots in Classical Greece and Rome, was a major force behind the Renaissance.

Mural A wall painting.

Patron A person who supports artists either by requesting or buying works of art on the open market.

Perspective The art of drawing objects on a flat surface so as to give the appearance of reality.

Index

Note: Page numbers in *italics* refer to illustrations.

Books to Read

The World of Leonardo by R Wallace (Time-Life)
The Life and Times of Leonardo by Liana Bortolon (Hamlyn)
Leonardo da Vinci by L H Heydenreich (Allen & Unwin)
Leonardo da Vinci: An Account of his Development as an Artist by Kenneth Clark (Penguin)
Leonardo da Vinci by L Goldscheider (Phaidon)
Leonardo da Vinci: The Tragic Pursuit of Perfection by A Valletin (W H Allen)
Lives of the Artists by G Vasari (Penguin)
The World of Leonardo da Vinci by I B Hart (Macdonald)
The Drawings of Leonardo da Vinci by A E Popham (Jonathan Cape)
Leonardo da Vinci and the Art of Science by Kenneth Keele (Priory Press)
The Inventions of Leonardo da Vinci by Charles Gibbs-Smith (Phaidon)

Acknowledgements

Picture Research : Jackie Cookson
Photographs: Ashmolean Museum, Oxford 15 *bottom;* Biblioteca Ambrosiana, Milan 16 *bottom right,* 22 *centre right, bottom left,* 23 *bottom;* British Museum, London 10 *centre;* Cleveland Museum of Art/The Holden Collection 4–5; Cliches Musees Nationaux, Paris 15 *top right,* 18 *bottom left,* 21 *right,* 25 *bottom left;* Corvina Archives, Budapest 18 *top left;* Mansell Collection 7, 14 *top left;* Mary Evans Picture Library 22 *centre left;* National Gallery of Art, Washington 13 *left;* Royal Collection, Windsor Castle, reproduced by Gracious Permission of Her Majesty The Queen 20 *top, centre left, bottom,* 24; SCALA/Bargello, Florence 13 *right;* SCALA/ Biblioteca Reale, Turin 25 *bottom right;* SCALA/Carmine Cupp Branacci 12; SCALA/Czartorisky, Museum, Cracow 17; SCALA/Gabinetto Disegni 10 *centre,* 16 *bottom left;* SCALA/Palazzo Vecchio, Florence 18 *bottom right;* SCALA/Santa Maria delle Grazie, Milan 2–3; SCALA/ Santa Trinita 14 *bottom;* SCALA/Uffizi, Florence 11, 15 *top left,* 16 *top;* Science Museum 9, 20 *centre right,* 22 *bottom right,* 23 *top;* ZEFA 15 *centre left.*